HAPPY CATS

summersdale

HAPPY CATS

An Hachette UK Company
www.hachette.co.uk

Summersdale Publishers Ltd
Part of Octopus Publishing Group Limited
Carmelite House
50 Victoria Embankment
LONDON
EC4Y 0DZ
UK

www.summersdale.com

Printed and bound in the Czech Republic

ISBN: 978-1-78685-277-9

Substantial discounts on bulk quantities of Summersdale books are available to corporations, professional associations and other organisations. For details contact general enquiries: telephone: +44 (0) 1243 771107 or email: enquiries@summersdale.com.

TO...

FROM.....................................

TRYING TO SING ALONG TO YOUR FAVOURITE SONG LIKE:

THIS UNDERFLOOR HEATING IS THE SHIZ.

GOOD MORNING, HUMAN.
WHAT DO YOU MEAN,
'WATCHING YOU IN
YOUR SLEEP'?

That would be creepy...

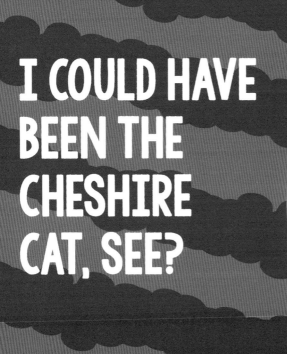

I COULD HAVE BEEN THE CHESHIRE CAT, SEE?

Pout is on point.

xoxox

But this *is* my pretty smile.

A tiny pillow
for a tiny cat.

SUGAR RUSSHHHHHHH!

lick
lick

SO.
MUCH.
TUNA.

NEW YEAR,

NEW ME.

Two days later...

I am happy.

THIS IS JUST
MY FACE.

Well Done

Hands up if you just peed on the new white rug!

Kitties
in love.
Awww.

Do you want to feed me now?

YOU WANT ME
TO BE HAPPY?
THEN GET ME A
COMFY BED.

What cat?
ALL I SEE IS A CUSHION.

Plié,
jeté,
slay!

#SpeedDemon

Gallop

like no one is
watching you.

IT'S CALLED FASHION, DARLING.

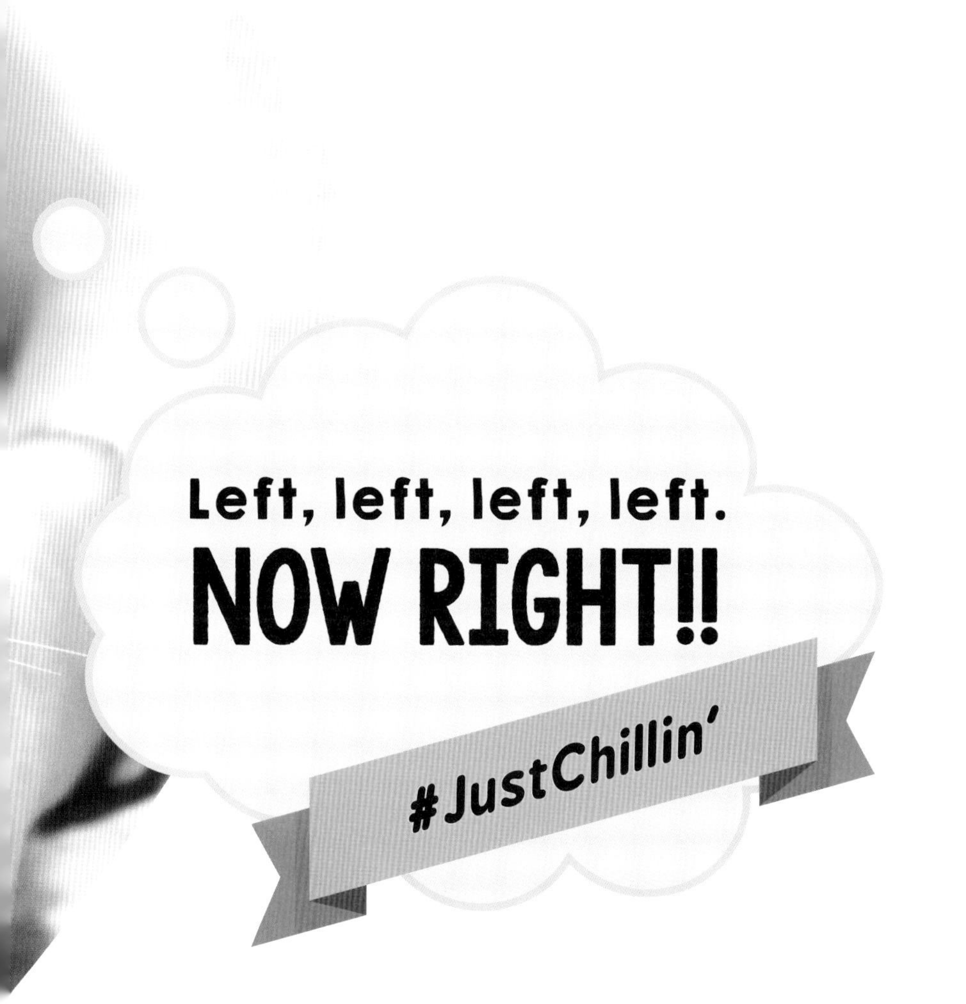
Left, left, left, left.
NOW RIGHT!!
#JustChillin'

DOING MY BEST
IMPRESSION OF A
PRAYING MANTIS.

THE MORNING AFTER

SASSY

IS MY MIDDLE NAME.

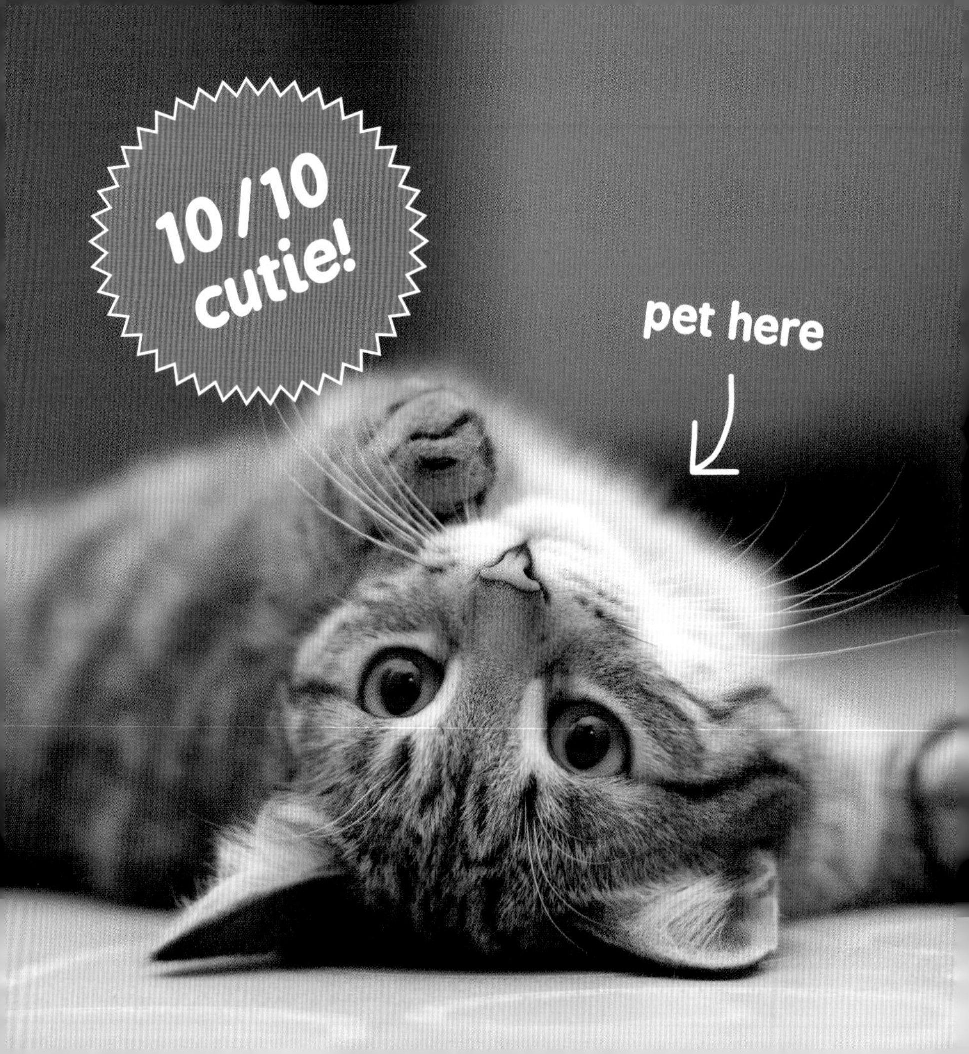
10/10 cutie!
pet here

**11.00 A.M.
Do some
cat yoga.**

OOPS!

I just let one slip!

#SorryNotSorry

Before one can yowl at the moon...

... one must meowl at the sun.

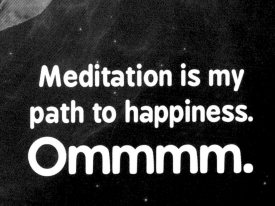

Meditation is my path to happiness. Ommmm.

AH, THE GOOD VIBES WEEKEND.

Such a big
stretch
for such a
tiny me.

If you're interested in finding out more
about our books, find us on Facebook
at Summersdale Publishers and follow
us on Twitter at @Summersdale.

www.summersdale.com